California's Missions

from

A to Z

By: Matt Weber

Copyright © 2010 - Matt Weber
www.121publications.com
ISBN-13: 978-0-9841931-9-6

The missions were the foundation for the Spanish colonization of an area that now includes modern-day California. Twenty-one missions were built near the coast from San Diego to the San Francisco Bay Area. They are the origin of many cities, names, agricultural products, roads, and architectural features in California. The purpose of the missions was to convert the native peoples to Catholicism and Spanish culture while establishing settlements in the territory.

This book uses the alphabet as a framework for exploring twenty-six historical and architectural features shared by the missions. This is not a definitive guide to each mission individually, but a thorough introduction to the California missions as a whole.

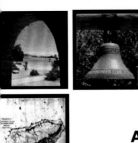

Table of Contents

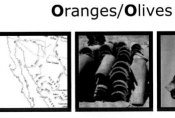

Arches are a major part
of mission design,
an architectural feature
in a single-file line.
Across the mission's front
and built into the towers,
the arcade blocks the sun
and shields from the showers.

Arches are the most recognizable architectural feature of the missions. The missions had arches of the Roman (half-round) style. The pillars were typically square. Arches allowed the missions to have outdoor corridors along their outside walls, without being fully enclosed. The arches supported the roof, which was extended out farther than the walls. This kept the mission buildings shaded from the sun and protected people from the sun and rain.

Some famous buildings in California that incorporate the mission architectural style are Stanford University, Hearst Castle, and many train depots, such as those in San Diego, Burlingame, and San Juan Capistrano. At Mission Santa Ines and Mission San Luis Rey, original arches have been left intact for visitors to see.

Bells were rung at missions
every single day,
ringing out a notice
heard from far away.
Signaling when to work
and when to pray and eat,
special bells today
represent a famous street.

Mission bells were used to signal when to work, eat, attend church, and sleep. They were also used to announce visitors and for special occasions. Many bells were first hung on wooden beams outside because the original churches were small and primitive. Depending on mission design, bells were located in a tower (belfry/campanile) or in a wall (campanario).

The first bells were cast in New Spain (Mexico) and brought to California by ship. Bells were blessed in special ceremonies, and they were cast with the date. Mission San Gabriel has a bell that weighs one ton and can be heard from 8 miles away. San Buenaventura has two wooden bells. Many missions still have one or more of their original bells.

Bells were placed as symbolic markers along the original route of El Camino Real (page 13).

Crosses were erected
at the end of every search,
to find the perfect place
to build a mission **church**.
Padres wanted Indians
to turn over a new leaf;
crosses are symbolic
of the priests' belief.

All of the missions have crosses. The cross is a symbol of the Catholic faith. Santa Cruz means "Holy Cross" or "Sacred Cross." In Carmel, a large wooden cross is in the quadrangle, recreated on the site where fragments of the cross erected by Junipero Serra were discovered during the mission restoration. Santa Clara has a tall cross erected in 1777. Now in protective casing, it stands across from the church entrance.

Churches were where religious services were held. Mission San Juan Bautista has the largest church of all the 21 missions. Mission Santa Barbara and Carmel are known for their recognizable stone churches. Mission San Luis Obispo has an L shaped church. Mission San Francisco de Asis's church is the oldest building in San Francisco.

D

Diego, San Diego,
the place saw Serra stand.
In 1769,
it's where it all began.
Twenty more would follow,
stretching up the coast.
Carmel was founded second.
Serra liked it most.

Mission San Diego was the first mission founded in Alta California. It was founded on July 16, 1769, when Father Serra raised a cross and held Mass. After travelling north to the Monterey Bay, he founded a second mission, San Carlos Boromeo (Carmel), on June 3, 1770. The last mission, San Francisco Solano, was founded July 4, 1823. In all, 21 missions were founded in Alta California between 1769 to 1823.

Mission San Diego's history is one that reflects much of what happened to many of the missions. Early on, it was moved to a better location. Mission San Diego also experienced a Native American revolt. The mission fell into ruin as the years passed, but was restored in the 20th century.

El Camino Real

linked the mission chain. "The Royal Road" was named to honor the king of Spain. When you left a mission and walked along this way, you'd get to another one in just about a day.

El Camino Real is the road, or path, that connected the missions in Alta California. In Spanish, it literally means "The Road Royal." From San Diego to San Francisco, it is approximately 600 miles long. Today, much of the original El Camino Real route is the same that Highway 101 follows, as well as part of Interstate 5, and Highway 82. There is a portion of the original El Camino Real next to Mission San Juan Bautista.

Between 1906 and 1913, 450 bell markers were installed along the route of El Camino Real. Most of these were lost, and there was a sporadic effort to replace them. Then, between 2000 and 2006, California's Highway Department (Caltrans) installed 555 bells along the route as part of a federal grant.

F

Fountains could be found at almost every mission, located in the gardens in a centralized position. Sometimes they're Italian or Moorish in their styles, sometimes using water channeled over miles.

Many of the missions had fountains in front, or within their courtyards. Although they were not always a necessary feature, they added to the beauty of the mission design. Some were circular, and others were in an octagon or star-like shape. The fountains' design was affected by Spanish, Italian, and Moorish cultures. Mission San Fernando Rey still has its original flower-shaped fountain in its courtyard. Mission San Luis Obispo has a fountain in front with a Native American girl and bears, because it is located in the Valley of the Bears. Missions San Juan Capistrano, Santa Barbara, San Miguel, and Carmel have large fountains that are often photographed. The fountain at Mission Santa Barbara is over 200 years old, built in 1808.

G

Gardens are a part
of many missions' grounds.
Buzzing bees, humming birds
make frequent garden sounds.
Growing herbs and spices,
fruits and flowers too,
Mediterranean plants
in the western climate grew.

Gardens were found in the inner courtyard of the missions, where there were pathways that connected the buildings and workshops. This created the opportunity for a location where a variety of plants were grown, many introduced to California from Spain and other places. It was convenient to have some fruit trees without needing to visit orchards. Plants such as herbs and spices were readily available and could be used fresh for cooking. Plants such as roses and other flowers were planted for decoration.

The current garden at La Purisima was created by adding plants from each of the other twenty missions' gardens. Mission San Juan Capistrano's garden is one of the most photographed and painted of all the missions.

Hides were quite important to the mission economy, used for leather there or sold clandestinely. For candles they used tallow better known as cow fat, collected from the cattle and boiled in a vat.

Cow hides were one of the most important goods produced for export by the missions. They were tanned and sold to be made into leather products. California's wide expanses of open pasture proved to be ideal for the raising of cattle. Hides were used so commonly in trade with visiting foreign ships that they earned the nickname "Yankee dollars." Trading with foreign ships was originally forbidden. However, out of necessity, the missions turned to trading with other countries. This was often done clandestinely (secretly).

The cows' fat, or tallow, was used for making candles. It was also sold or traded to ships to be sold to soap factories abroad. Tallow candles were a cheaper alternative to beeswax candles.

Independence was disruptive when it came. It meant that mission life would never be the same. Secularization meant no more a helping hand. Missions could be churches, but had to sell their land.

In 1810, people in Mexico declared independence from Spain. In 1821, Mexico became an independent country. Little changed for the missions, except they were then allowed to trade with foreign countries. In 1834, however, the Mexican government officially secularized the missions. This meant that the missions would receive no financial aid from the government and had to be self-supporting. The mission lands were sold or given away in land grants. Many of the mission buildings were not maintained and began to deteriorate. In 1863, Abraham Lincoln signed a law to return the missions to the Catholic church. Most were in disrepair and continued to deteriorate. What is seen today, is the result of rebuilding or significant restoration.

J

Junipero Serra is
the man who's famous for
the starting of nine missions,
followed by twelve more.
People in California
were without God, he heard.
He started founding missions
so he could spread the Word.

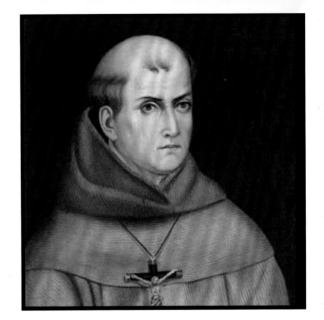

Junipero Serra was the Spanish priest (padre) who was in charge of establishing missions in Alta California. He traveled with Gaspar de Portola, founding Mission San Diego. They then located Monterey Bay and founded Mission San Carlos Borromeo. Serra oversaw the founding of nine missions in California before his death. Fermin Lausen, his successor, founded nine more.

Junipero Serra was born on November 24, 1713, and died at 70 on August 28, 1784. During his lifetime, he lived in Spain, Mexico City, Baja California, and Alta California. Today, there are many statues of Junipero Serra at the missions. There is a large statue located on Highway 280, the Junipero Serra Freeway.

Kitchens were busy places at the missions every day. Wood was burned for heat in ovens made of clay. Cooks were busily making meals from food they grew, like tortillas, atole, and beef and veggie stew.

The missions had a variety of kitchens for cooking the mission meals. The "bee-hive" oven, or hornito, was a common fixture in outdoor kitchens. The missions would have outdoor kitchens to reduce the risk of fire and the unpleasantness of smoke indoors. Later, as the designs were able to adapt to these problems, the missions built kitchens indoors. Often there would be a wood-burning oven in the corner, along with places for pots to be placed on or hung over coals. Some kitchens were made with a pass-through to the dining room. Mission meals were usually simple, consisting often of atole (cornmeal porridge), tortillas, some meat, and seasonal fruits and vegetables. There was also a sweet and thick hot chocolate called champurrado.

Lavanderia was where
at missions could be seen,
a rectangular water basin
for washing clothing clean.
Reservoirs held water, too,
for months when it was drier.
They pooled water from
locations that were higher.

The lavanderia was the wash basin for the missions, from the Spanish word lavar, to wash. The missions brought water via aquaduct to large rectangular basins that were lined with stones or bricks and mortar. The design would sometimes include a bumpy side for washing the clothes and an embankment with sun exposure for drying the clothes. Some of the more elaborate ones had the water enter through a spigot, a gargoyle, or a carved stone figure. Kiln-fired bricks would be used. They are more waterproof than regular adobe.

San Luis Rey has a beautiful well-restored lavanderia. Santa Barbara has a well-known figurehead on its lavanderia that has been considered to be the first public sculpture in California. La Purisima has a circular lavanderia.

M

Monterey was a place
the sailors liked the best,
a calm bay where to anchor,
so ships could safely rest.
A mission, town, and fort
were built upon the shore.
And it was the capital,
in 1794.

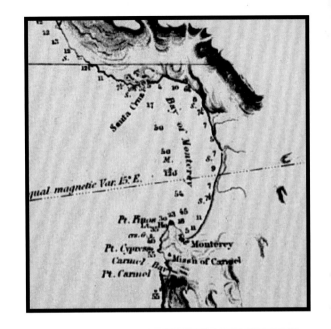

Monterey was the capital of Alta California from 1777 until 1849. Mission Carmel, which was the headquarters for the Alta California missions, was founded at Monterey Bay. It was later relocated farther away from the presidio and town.

Monterey Bay is one of the largest navigable bays in California. Spain put presidios, or forts, at the most important navigable and protected harbors in Alta California, at Monterey, San Diego, Santa Barbara, and San Francisco. When the French-Argentinean pirate Hippolyte de Bouchard attacked Spanish California, it was Monterey and Mission Carmel where he first struck. In 1846, when American troops claimed California during the Mexican-American war, it was in Monterey where they landed ships and raised the American flag.

Native Americans were the reason for the missions. The padres wanted Catholics with Spanish traditions. Neophytes were put to work and sometimes felt like slaves. Many died of illnesses and went to early graves.

Native Americans were the original inhabitants, or indigenous people, of California. The entire purpose of the missions was to convert the existing inhabitants of California into Spanish citizens. This required teaching the Native Americans the Catholic religion and Spanish culture. The neophytes, or newly converted, were expected to give up their old ways of life and adopt Spanish language, food, agriculture, clothes, and crafts. The Native Americans supplied almost all the manual labor in the construction of the missions and in the production of goods that the missions produced for self-sufficiency and trade. The treatment of the Native Americans, and the coercion they suffered, varied by who was in charge at the different missions or presidios.

Olives and also **O**ranges
are crops the missions grew.
The Spanish introduced them,
with grapes and pepper too.
Transforming California
in a major way,
some trees that they planted
can still be found today.

The Spanish padres introduced many plants to California, such as olive, orange, pepper, fig, and pomegranate trees, that are now found all over the state. They also planted the first vineyards in California. The first wine grapes and wine were produced at San Juan Capistrano in 1779. The first pepper tree in California is located at San Luis Rey, planted in 1830. The olive tree in front of San Antonio was planted in 1836. The olive trees behind Mission Santa Clara are from the 1820's. The first orange groves in California were planted at Mission San Gabriel in 1804. Cuttings from plants were used to begin new plants in other locations. Spain and California are both located in areas that experience the "Mediterranean Climate." This meant that many plants that were familiar to the Spanish were able to grow in California.

Padre was the priest or "father" at each site, instructing all the people every day and night. In sandals and a robe a deeply religious man, working at a mission far from his native land.

The padres founded and ran the missions. Juan Crespi, a close friend of Junipero Serra, was in charge of Mission San Diego and is buried in Carmel near to Serra.

Father Pedro Estevan Tapis was famous for taking over as father presidente, or president, of the missions after Lasuen. He also founded Mission Santa Ines (19th in the chain). He also worked at San Juan Bautista establishing a renowned music teaching system and singing choir.

Narciso Duran was the "president" three times for a total of 13 years, between 1824 and 1846. Mariano Payeras was the "president" for 5 years and visited all 20 missions. Vicente Francisco de Sarria was also the "president" and founded San Rafael.

Quadrangle is the shape
of a central courtyard where
the walls of four buildings
create a middle square.
Central to each mission,
a shape the missions share,
if they were attacked,
it was safer inside there.

Most of the missions were arranged in a square shape called a quadrangle. Spain mandated it to be done this way. The quadrangle design located narrow buildings near each other for easy access and gave the mission a more secure layout. The mission church was often on one side of the quadrangle. The other sides held rooms of various purposes, such as the padres' rooms and the dormitories. Other sides held the workshops for candle making, weaving, carpentry, etc. Often there was a chapel. Kitchens were in a room or in the courtyard, or a combination of both. Sometimes there were soldiers' rooms. When Mission La Purisima rebuilt after the 1812 earthquake, it was arranged in a linear design. It is the exception to the typical quadrangle design of the missions.

Rivers were important for every mission site. Sometimes using aqueducts which were water-tight. Cooking, crops, cleaning, and quenching people's thirst, before they founded missions, fresh water was found first.

Fresh water was a critical element in choosing a mission location. Missions were located near rivers or springs to provide water for drinking, washing, livestock, plants, and farming. Water also provided a power source for mills at some missions. Missions San Antonio, San Buenaventura, San Diego, San Luis Obispo, San Luis Rey, and Santa Ines all have rivers that share the same name as the mission. Mission Santa Clara was located near the Guadalupe River, the same on which the pueblo of San Jose was located. San Carlos Borromeo del Rio Carmelo is commonly referred to as Carmel because that was the name of the river and the bay, as well as the current city and beach. San Francisco de Asis is often called Mission Dolores because Dolores was the name of the nearby stream and lake.

S

Saints are holy people
they're famous and acclaimed.
To honor famous saints,
missions were often named.
Some named for a woman,
others for a man,
Santa goes with Clara,
but Miguel starts with San.

Many of the missions are named after Christian saints. San Diego de Alcala means Saint Didacus of Alcala. San Carlos Borromeo means Saint Charles Borromeo. San Antonio is Saint Anthony. San Gabriel Arcangel is Saint Gabriel the Archangel. San Luis Obispo is Saint Louis (the) Bishop. Francisco de Asis is Francis of Assisi. Juan is John and Clara is Claire. San Buenaventura is Saint Bonaventure, and Santa Barbara is Saint Barbara. La Purisima Conception means The Pure (immaculate) Conception. Santa Cruz means Sacred Cross. Nuestra Senora de Soledad means Our Lady of Solitude. Juan Bautista is John the Baptist. Miguel is Michael and Ines is Agnes. Fernando Rey and Luis Rey are King Ferdinand and King Louis (the saints). Rafael is Raphael and Francisco Solano is Francis Solanus.

Tiles are found upon
each roof way up high,
a curved red clay shape
as though over a man's thigh.
To funnel rain and fire-proof
are reasons to use tile,
nowadays architecturally
to copy mission style.

Tile roofs are one of the most recognizable features of mission design and architecture. The first mission buildings did not have tile roofs. Their roofs were made of thatch (woven vegetation). In 1776, much of Mission San Luis Obispo was destroyed by a fire that started from a flaming arrow during an attack. Tile roofs became the standard for the missions for protection from fire (accidental and intentional). The tile roofs also helped to protect the adobe walls from weathering. Both San Luis Obispo and Mission San Antonio de Padua are credited with being the first to make and use clay tiles.

While it is possible to shape the tiles over one's thigh, the missions used a rectangular or trapezoidal mold to create the tiles and a smoothed log for shaping them.

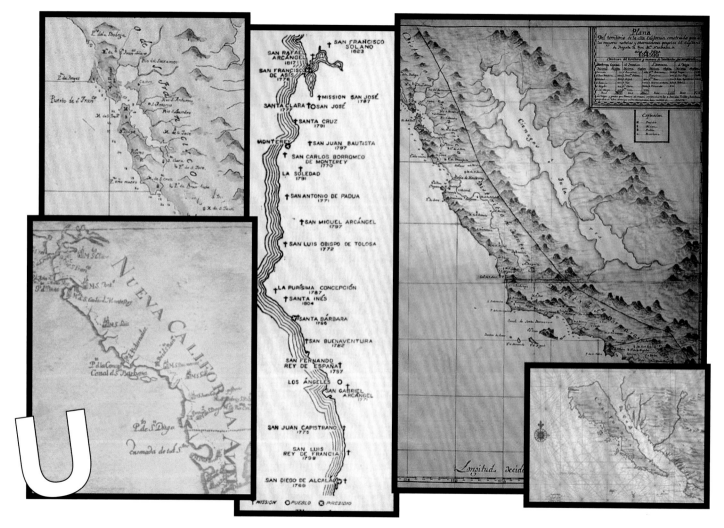

Upper translates to Alta
in case you didn't know.
Baja's the peninsula
located down below.
Alta California
is where we are today,
missions from San Diego
to San Francisco Bay.

When California was claimed by Spain, it was called Alta California which means Upper California. California, as it is geographically defined today, had a total of 21 missions. There were also many missions in Baja, or "Lower," California. The Alta California missions were founded by the Franciscan order of the Catholic church. In Baja California, 29 missions were founded by the Jesuits and the Dominicans. Two Baja missions were founded by the Franciscans in 1769. Spain also had missions in Texas, Arizona, New Mexico, and Florida.

California is named after a mythical island in a popular Spanish book of the time. When the first explorers discovered Baja California, navigating only its southern end, they thought that it was an island. Further exploration revealed that it was a long peninsula.

V

Vaqueros were the men
who roped and branded cattle,
skilled with their reatas,
they rode tall in the saddle.
They bundled hides and tallow
and barbequed the rest.
California's "cowboys" were
the first ones in the West.

Vaquero, or cowboy, comes from the Spanish word vaca, or cow. Because cattle hides were such an important industry to the missions, many Native American men learned to be vaqueros. At roundup time, they lassoed the cows and either branded or slaughtered them. They used reatas, ropes of braided leather, for the lassoing. After slaughtering, they needed to process the hide and tallow for sale. When California's settled areas were converted into ranchos, many of the Native American mission vaqueros found work at the ranchos. Each mission had a distinct brand that signified that certain cows belonged to them. Missions and ranchos did not use fences, so livestock would be intermingled until roundup time when they would be sorted. A calf without a brand could be identified by its mother's brand.

47

Walking was a common way to get from place to place. Each mission was a day apart if you kept a steady pace. Sailing up the coast by ship was another way you know. San Francisco was three days north from San Diego.

Each mission in California was approximately 30-40 miles apart from each other, which is about a one-day walk. Travelers would go by foot, horseback, or oxen-drawn cart, called a carreta. Legend has it that the padres would carry mustard seeds as they traveled so that their path would be easier to follow in the future. The wild mustard plants now seen over much of California's open space near where they would have walked is said to have come from them. They were also known to carve crosses on large trees along the way. There is one such tree on display at Mission San Miguel. There is an actual cross on a hill above the city of Ventura that Father Serra had erected in 1782 as a landmark to help travelers find Mission San Buenaventura.

eXplorers were the men
to go searching for the king,
for harbors, land, and rivers
that were good for settling.
Anza and Portola are
two that earned great fame.
They traveled with the padres
in case some danger came.

Explorers traveled with the padres to help protect them and to help settle the land. Many years earlier, explorers traveled by ship to map the new lands. Spanish officials and priests used the maps and prior information to decide where they wanted to place the first missions and presidios. The explorers were usually officers in the Spanish military.

Juan Rodriguez Cabrillo and Sebastian Viscaino were the first Spanish explorers to map and report about the Alta California coast. Gaspar de Portola traveled with Junipero Serra to found missions and presidios at San Diego and Monterey. Juan Bautista de Anza traveled across deserts to California and explored the San Francisco Bay Area. Juan Manuel de Ayala was the first explorer to sail into San Francisco Bay.

Yerba Buena was a pueblo,
San Francisco it's today,
a village near the mission
and the fort not far away.
Another Spanish pueblo
was the town of San Jose.
Perhaps you know another,
that we now call L.A.

In addition to the missions and presidios, Spain established three pueblos, or small towns. These were established as agricultural settlements. San Jose was established first in 1777 with 14 families that moved from Mexico. Los Angeles was founded with 44 families in 1781. The pueblo of Branciforte was established in 1797 and later became part of the city of Santa Cruz. Under Mexican rule, a pueblo was established at Sonoma. In 1820, there were 976 people living in the pueblos of San Jose, Los Angeles, and Branciforte.

The communities at each presidio were later classified as pueblos. These were the pueblos of San Diego, Yerba Buena (San Francisco), Monterey, and Santa Barbara. Yerba Buena means "good herb" in Spanish, named after the wild mint found there.

Z

JUANA MARIA
INDIAN WOMAN ABANDONED ON
SAN NICOLAS ISLAND EIGHTEEN YEARS
FOUND AND BROUGHT TO
SANTA BARBARA
BY
CAPT. GEORGE NIDEVER
IN 1853

Zia is a girl
4th graders might know well,
a story about the missions
written by Scott O'Dell.
A Native American girl
at the Santa Barbara Mission,
a Newbery book sequel,
history mixed with fiction.

Scott O'Dell won the Newbery Award (distinguished children's literature) for the historical fiction book, *Island of the Blue Dolphins*. It is the story of an Indian girl named Karana, who lives alone for many years on San Nicolas Island.

Zia, published in 1976, is a historical fiction story that takes place during the mission period. It is about Karana's niece, named Zia, who lives at Mission Santa Barbara. The book describes what life at the missions felt like from a Native American perspective. It also answers the question of "What happened to Karana?"

Visitors to Mission Santa Barbara can see a plaque honoring Juana Maria (Karana), who was buried in the mission cemetery in 1853.

Photograph/Illustration Locations Reference Index

	Left side full-page	Right side square	Other
A	San Juan Bautista	San Antonio de Padua	
B	San Juan Bautista	San Juan Bautista	101 by Pismo Beach
C	Santa Barbara	San Francisco de Asis	
D	San Diego	San Diego	
E	San Juan Bautista	Hwy. 101	
F	San Juan Capistrano	Santa Barbara	
G	Santa Barbara	San Carlos Borromeo (Carmel)	
H	San Juan Bautista	San Juan Bautista	San Antonio de Padua
I	San Juan Capistrano	San Diego	
J	Statue at San Juan Bautista	Junipero Serra	Hwy. 280
K	San Carlos Borromeo (Carmel)	San Juan Bautista	
L	San Antonio de Padua	Santa Barbara	
M	Monterey Customs House	Monterey Bay	Customs House
N	San Antonio de Padua	Chumash Painted Cave St. Park	Chumash Canoe
O	San Antonio de Padua	San Carlos Borromeo (Carmel)	
P	California's first baptism	Santa Barbara	Santa Barbara
Q	San Francisco de Asis (model)	San Juan Capistrano	
R	San Antonio de Padua aquaduct	San Antonio de Padua	
S	Santa Barbara's museum	San Carlos Borromeo (Carmel)	
T	San Antonio de Padua	San Antonio de Padua	
U	various old California maps	Baja California	
V	historical art by Smyth & Walker	cow	Carmel's museum
W	South San Jose	Franciscan padres	
X	Monterey Bay	Juan Bautista de Anza	
Y	San Francisco Presidio	Pueblo San Jose (stamp)	
Z	Santa Barbara	San Nicolas Island	Santa Barbara cemetery

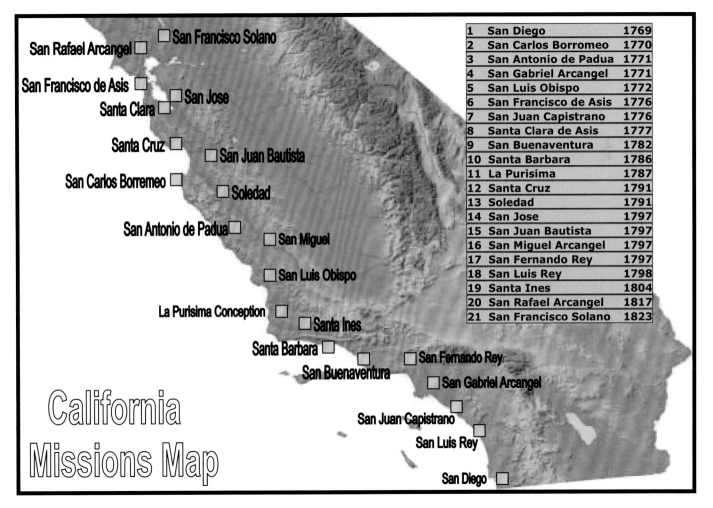

California Missions Map

1	San Diego	1769
2	San Carlos Borromeo	1770
3	San Antonio de Padua	1771
4	San Gabriel Arcangel	1771
5	San Luis Obispo	1772
6	San Francisco de Asis	1776
7	San Juan Capistrano	1776
8	Santa Clara de Asis	1777
9	San Buenaventura	1782
10	Santa Barbara	1786
11	La Purisima	1787
12	Santa Cruz	1791
13	Soledad	1791
14	San Jose	1797
15	San Juan Bautista	1797
16	San Miguel Arcangel	1797
17	San Fernando Rey	1797
18	San Luis Rey	1798
19	Santa Ines	1804
20	San Rafael Arcangel	1817
21	San Francisco Solano	1823

Answers to Mission Report Questions   Name: _____

A	
B	
C	
D	
E	
F	
G	
H	
I	
J	
K	
L	
M	
N	
O	
P	
Q	
R	
S	
T	
U	
V	
W	
X	
Y	
Z	

One possible mission report format is to use the A to Z topics as questions about a specific mission. After choosing a mission to study, see if the information can be found that answers the questions in the following 26 categories. If your mission report answers all (or most) of these questions, it will be an excellent and thorough report.

Arches	How many arches does your mission have? What does the front look like?
Bells	How many bells does your mission have? How many are original?
Crosses	When was your mission founded? (the first cross raised to mark the location)
Diego	What number was your mission founded?
El Camino	What number is it located, north from San Diego?
Fountain	Is there anything interesting about a fountain at your mission?
Gardens	Is there anything interesting about your mission's garden?
Hides	What does the brand for your mission look like?
Independence	When was your mission secularized? When was it restored?
Junipero	Who founded your mission?
Kitchen	What did they eat at your mission?
Lavenderia	What were the jobs that Native American women had at your mission?
Monterey	What presidio district is your mission in?
Native Americans	What was the tribe that was at your mission?
Olive/Oranges	What were some of the crops that your mission grew?
Padres	What were the names of some of the padres at your mission?
Quadrangle	What buildings of your mission are currently there?
River	What was the river or source of fresh water for your mission?
Saints	What does your mission's name mean?
Tiles	What were the jobs that Native American men had at your mission?
Upper	What are the missions that are geographically closest to your mission?
Vaquero	How many of each type of livestock were at your mission?
Walking	How far away from where you live is your mission?
e**X**plorers	Which explorer, if any, visited the coast or lands near your mission first?
Yerba Buena	What is the pueblo that was closest to your mission? What city is your mission in now?
Zia	Are there any books about your mission, both fictional and non-fiction?

This book is dedicated to Caitlin and Samantha

Special thanks to my 4th grade teachers Mr. Paige and Mrs. Andrews, as well my colleagues Jo Ann Gillespie and Heidi Pierce,

Cover design by Megan Gillespie

Special thanks to Jeffrey Han, Ken Marks,
David McLaughlin, and Debbie Self for their help.

Visit **121publications.com** for more information about this book and other books by **Matt Weber.**

If you enjoyed this book, you may also enjoy **San Francisco – The Alphabet Book**, which takes readers on an alphabetic journey through the sights and history of San Francisco.